No Girls Allowed

Kids Can Press acknowledges the financial support of the Government of Ontario, through the Ontario Media Development Corporation's Ontario Book Initiative; the Ontario Arts Council; the Canada Council for the Arts; and the Government of Canada, through the BPIDP, for our publishing activity.

Published in Canada by
Kids Can Press Ltd.
25 Dockside Drive
Toronto, ON M5A 0B5

Published in the U.S. by
Kids Can Press Ltd.
2250 Military Road
Tonawanda, NY 14150

www.kidscanpress.com

Edited by Stacey Roderick and Karen Li
Designed by Marie Bartholomew

The hardcover edition of this book is smyth sewn casebound.
The paperback edition of this book is limp sewn with a drawn-on cover.
Manufactured in Buji, Shenzhen, China, in 2/2011 by WKT Company

CM 08 0 9 8 7 6 5 4 3 2 1
CM PA 08 0 9 8 7 6 5 4 3 2

Library and Archives Canada Cataloguing in Publication

Hughes, Susan, 1960-
    No girls allowed : tales of daring women dressed as men for love, freedom and adventure / Susan Hughes ; Willow Dawson, illustrator.

Interest age level: Ages 9-12 years.
ISBN 978-1-55453-177-6 (bound). ISBN 978-1-55453-178-3 (pbk.)

1. Male impersonators—Biography—Juvenile literature. 2. Transgender people—Biography—Juvenile literature. 3. Transvestites—Biography—Juvenile literature. I. Dawson, Willow II. Title.

HQ76.97.H84 2008   j306.77'80820922   C2007-906084-6

No Girls Allowed

Tales of Daring Women Dressed as Men for Love, Freedom and Adventure

Written by
Susan Hughes

Illustrated by
Willow Dawson

Kids Can Press

To sweet Fiona, who asked to hear the stories — S.H.

This book is for you, Dad. Thank you for teaching me how to draw,
how to play a saw and, most importantly, that girls are allowed!
Special thanks to my husband, Ray, and to Karen L., Susan, Marie, Karen B.
and the rest of the KCP gang — W.D.

Contents

Hatshepsut......................7

Mu Lan......................20

Alfhild......................28

Esther Brandeau............38

James Barry..................49

Ellen Craft....................61

Sarah Rosetta Wakeman....68

Afterword......................78

Further Reading......................80

Hatshepsut

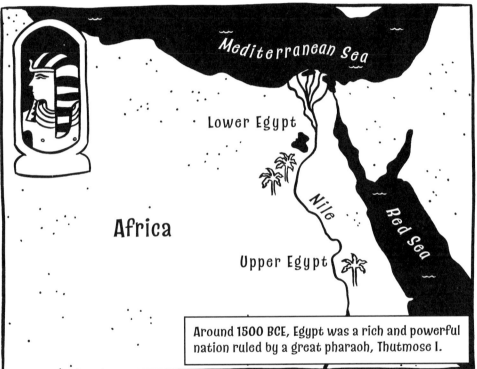

Around 1500 BCE, Egypt was a rich and powerful nation ruled by a great pharaoh, Thutmose I.

Thutmose I treated his only daughter, Hatshepsut, very well. Unlike other girls of this time, she grew up knowing a lot about politics and power.

The royal line of a pharaoh could be confusing. He could have a great wife, who was queen, plus one or more minor wives.

The men hold the power. Yet it's women who carry the royal blood. My daughter can never be pharaoh, but someday her son may be.

THUTMOSE 1
Pharaoh

AAHMES
Great Wife

MOUTNOFRIT
Minor Wife

I may only be a minor wife, but if my son, Akheperenre, marries Hatshepsut, he may be pharaoh one day.

WADJMOSE

AMENMOSE

One of Hatshepsut's two other brothers will likely be pharaoh. Their mother is his great wife.

AKHEPERENRE

HATSHEPSUT

Marry my half-brother, Akheperenre? Well, I don't have a choice. After all, I'm just a girl.

Soon after Hatshepsut married ...

First Wadjmose, then Amenmose. And now my father is dead.

So Hatshepsut's husband, Akheperenre, will be our new pharaoh?

Yes, though his health is not the best ...

Hatshepsut, a daughter, was not eligible for the throne.

And now, my brother and husband, you are the pharaoh, Thutmose II.

And you, my great wife, will reign with me. I will need your help!

Don't worry. You will have my help. Father trained me well.

COUGH! COUGH!

But Thutmose II was ill and died three years later. Because he and Hatshepsut had only a daughter, the next pharaoh would be the young son that Thutmose II had with Isis, his minor wife.

Hatshepsut, the baby's aunt and stepmother, was chosen to be the regent and to rule until Thutmose III was old enough to reign.

But she wanted more ...

11

13

Later that evening, Hatshepsut considered Senenmut's plan.

Will I be pharaoh, as my father was?

It is for the best.

She's dressed like a pharaoh!

The next time Hatshepsut appeared in public ...

We will spend less on war and more on trade and buildings — and the arts!

Your people will approve.

What are you making?

A new statue of Hatshepsut.

But she looks like a man!

Those are my orders.

I hear she has given up the title Great Wife.

I heard she's given her title of God's Wife of Amon to her daughter.

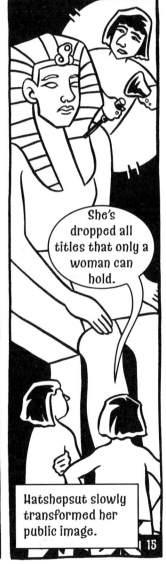

She's dropped all titles that only a woman can hold.

Hatshepsut slowly transformed her public image.

15

Several years passed. Hatshepsut decided that it was time.

Remember that Thutmose I loved Hatshepsut above her brothers. He wanted her to rule.

There is more. Thutmose I raised her and taught her well, but he is not her true father. Hatshepsut's true father is divine. He is the great god Amun.

This means that Hatshepsut, too, is divine.

Yes, this is so.

The High Priest of Amun says it is true!

GASP!

Hatshepsu is the masculine form of Hatshepsut.

During the 20 years the brave and ambitious Hatshepsu ruled, she built magnificent temples ...

... protected her country's borders

... and increased Egypt's wealth.

As Commander-in-Chief, you have become the most powerful general in my army, nephew.

He could seize power from Hatshepsut right now.

Perhaps his new title is enough for the time being.

About 15 years after Hatshepsu became pharaoh, her nephew grew old enough to take power. No one knows whether or not Hatshepsu gave up her throne voluntarily.

Around this time, Hatshepsu disappeared. She may have retired or perhaps died. Some even say she was murdered.

Hatshepsu's name was erased from many monuments and replaced with Thutmose III's name.

For centuries, no one knew the unacceptable truth that a woman had once been pharaoh – or where Hatshepsu's remains lay. In 2007, her mummy was finally identified in an unmarked tomb.

19

Mu Lan

Asia

Yellow River

Yangtze River

Around 1400 years ago, a poem was written in northern China. It recorded the legendary tale of a brave girl named Mu Lan. Her story continues to be told today.

Look, Mu Lan!

Oh, no. Messengers from the Khan!

The Khan was the powerful Mongolian ruler who governed a vast Asian Empire, including China.

When the Khan needed help fighting the tribes of Northern China, he drafted more soldiers into his army.

The Khan wants one male from each household.

To go to war could mean death for a brother, father or son.

Mu Lan, aren't you going to look?

Why? I have no brothers and my father is too old to fight.

Yes, and your father never lets anyone forget how much he'd prefer a son.

Mu Lan! My father's name is here! Your father's, too!

The Khan cannot expect my father to fight! He wouldn't survive the journey to meet the troops!

I must protect him somehow ...

21

Later that night, Mu Lan returned to her weaving. She was also weaving a plan ...

I will go in Father's place.

He can't fight anymore, not since his illness.

But the Khan's men don't have hearts, only swords. They could execute your father.

I've come up with a solution.

I'll say I am his son. All my youth, I've helped him train. I ride well. No one will suspect —

But for a girl to move among men so closely! It will bring dishonor.

To refuse the order will bring even greater dishonor.

Father won't object. I'm just a girl. I may as well be a ghost.

Good-bye, Father.

Wearing her father's armor, Mu Lan traveled 1000 lonely miles to join the army.

When she arrived, she gave her "brother's" name. No one questioned the boy with the lowered eyes who rode with confidence.

For years, Mu Lan fought alongside the other warriors. Battle after battle, she remained in disguise.

The other warriors respected their companion's bravery and skill in the martial arts. None of them guessed that the young man was not who he appeared to be.

The years passed. Mu Lan rose through the ranks, becoming a general.

Ten years after Mu Lan went to war ...

The war is over!

We can head home, General.

Yes, finally!

General, the Khan wishes to see you.

After many days of traveling, Mu Lan reached the capital city to be presented to the Khan.

General, I wish to reward you for your outstanding service with a high position in my government.

And continue in this disguise? And go longer without seeing my family?

Son of Heaven, thank you for this honor. However, I must decline. There is only one thing I desire.

Yes?

I wish to return home to my village, to my family, to a life of peace.

Mu Lan was happy to remove her armor and live as a woman again. But after some time, she received a letter ...

So my army companions have learned who I really am. They want to come and see me. Do they think I betrayed their trust?

It's true. She's a woman!

I ... I am pleased to greet you again.

Mu Lan, you are remarkable.

A fine daughter and an incredible warrior!

The famous poem does not explain how Mu Lan spent the rest of her days. But it ends with these words about Mu Lan's disguise ...

"Two hares running side by side close to the ground, How can they tell if I am he or she?"

Alfhild

In the 9th century, farmers and fishers lived peacefully in the kingdoms of Scandinavia. But there were also the Vikings, Scandinavian warriors and traders who sailed to other parts of Europe and North America to trade, raid and loot. At this time, there lived a beautiful princess.

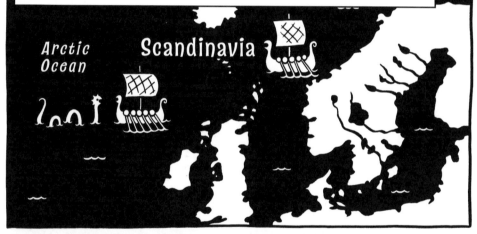

Arctic Ocean

Scandinavia

How are you this morning, Alfhild?

Fine, Mother.

Princess Alfhild, daughter of King Siward, was so beautiful that her parents kept her in a cabin, hidden from men.

And they didn't stop there.

I am Prince Alf, the son of the Danish king, Syragus.

I have come to see the daughter of Siward.

Sir, I don't advise that you ...

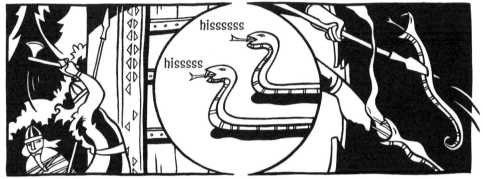

hissssss

hisssss

Sir, you have killed my vipers!

I apologize. It was the only way for me to win your hand in marriage!

29

That evening, Alfhild discussed Alf's proposal with her family.

So we're going to have a wedding!

Let's not be too hasty.

Son-in-law, those were the rules you set. Kill the vipers and win Alfhild in marriage.

Perhaps Alfhild doesn't want to marry the first brute to reach her cabin safely.

A Viking father usually consulted his daughter about her marriage wishes. King Siward, however, delayed ... and delayed ...

Give her some time to think about it.

Why? He's brave and strong ...

Just take some time to think.

First they lock me away. Then they go back on their promise.

Anything is better than being locked up day and night, even life on the open sea as a Viking.

It took some time for Alfhild to get her sea legs.

It was a hard life. The Vikings searched for goods to steal and then trade, or for food. Alfild often went hungry.

Eventually, she became a skilled sailor. She even joined in on the raids, despite the many dangers.

If I could be my own boss, find my own adventures, I might be happy living at sea.

Sometimes I do hate being disguised, though. And I miss having other women around ...

There *was* something about one of the other pirates, Groa.

34

Alfhild came up with a plan.

... so I propose that we form our own bandit gang. There are enough of us. And then we'll get to do things our way.

Stir things up a bit!

AYE! WE'RE WITH YOU, ALFHILD!

For several months, the new crew attacked other ships and raided villages along the coast. Soon Alfhild had a whole fleet of pirate ships.

Captain, ships to the west. They bear the royal crest of Denmark, and they're coming at us fast!

You know what I always say: when in doubt, ATTACK!

Despite being outnumbered, the determined leader and his crew boarded Alfhild's ship.

36

Unexpectedly reunited, Alf and Alfhild couldn't wait to get married. What adventures Alfhild got up to next, no one knows, but chances are she was never the well-behaved princess her parents hoped for!

Oh, my love!

It's you!

Esther Brandeau

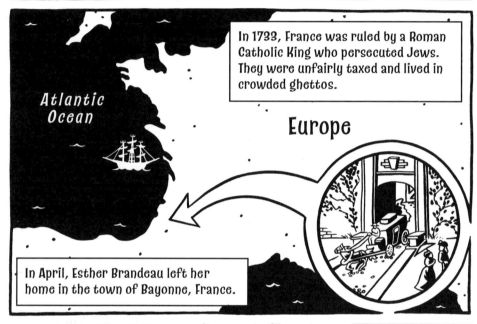

In 1732, France was ruled by a Roman Catholic King who persecuted Jews. They were unfairly taxed and lived in crowded ghettos.

Atlantic Ocean

Europe

In April, Esther Brandeau left her home in the town of Bayonne, France.

For so long the walls of the Jewish quarter have boxed me in, but today I leave.

Your aunt will meet you in Amsterdam. Write to me as soon as you arrive.

I will, Mama.

I'll miss you, Mama ...

JEWS! MAMA, LOOK!

Au revoir, Esther. Remember to follow God's commandments. Keep all the Jewish laws. You must not eat pork. You must not —

Papa, Papa, they are boarding!

Life there may hold more promise for you. Daughters must do as fathers say. And it is your father's wish that you go.

I will do as you say, Papa. *Au revoir!*

39

But that very night, Esther's ship ran aground ...

40

Hold on! We're almost there!

Madame Churiau, there has been a shipwreck and only two survivors. Monsieur Latour took in the sailor. Can you help this one?

Of course, of course! Bring the poor thing in right away.

Here. Some broth.

One week passed ...

Oh! You seem much better!

REM ... LLOW GOD'S COMMAND ... MENT ... EEP ALL JEWISH LAWS. YOU ... MUST NOT EAT PORK REM ... TO FOLLOW GOD'S COM MA ... MENTS. KEEP ALL JEWIS LA ... YOU MUST NOT EAT PORK. REME

What is this soup?

It is broth made from vegetables and the carcass of a pig.

Didn't you like it?

Yes. It was delicious. It's just that ... I can't explain.

Only half a day's journey from home!

Could you tell me where I am?

You are in the home of Madame Churiau in Biarritz.

Esther didn't try to find her way home. Perhaps she was ashamed of breaking the Jewish laws ...

Or perhaps she was getting a hint of what life could be like if only ...

Jews!

But I could do more for you. I know how to read and write.

So? You're just a girl. It doesn't matter what you know or what you think. We women only work our fingers to the bone, or get married, or both!

Or perhaps ...

I could face father, but I don't belong in the ghetto!

What if no one knew I was a girl? Are these breeches my chance for freedom?

43

Pierre Alansiette? You are the one that reads and writes?

Oui!

Hired. Come aboard.

And when we arrive, monsieur, we will expect to unload our cargo ...

Still disguised as Pierre, Esther worked next on a Spanish ship. After that, she would work in a number of French cities.

Read it again, boy. Then I will want to send a reply.

44

45

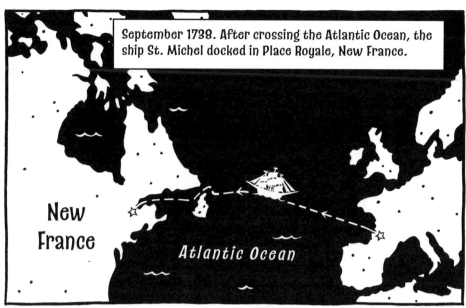

September 1738. After crossing the Atlantic Ocean, the ship St. Michel docked in Place Royale, New France.

New France

Atlantic Ocean

Everything is so different here. Maybe in this new land there is also more freedom for women.

Oh, it would be good to be able to be Esther Brandeau again!

But not complete freedom.

But only days after her arrival, Esther was dragged in front of Le Sieur Hocquart, Intendant of Quebec. She had been discovered.

This is the Jew?

But this is a woman!

Oui, Intendant Hocquart. It turns out Jacques La Farge is both a Jew and a woman!

Incredible. You must be the first Jewish woman on the shores of this land.

But what can we do with her? We can't send a woman, even one such as her, to the local jail.

Do you have anything to say for yourself? Did no one tell you that this is a colony for French Catholics?

47

It seems that Esther stayed in New France for about one year, living at a hospital and then in several private homes. She refused to be converted. The law said she had to be shipped back to France and tried at court. On September 27, 1739, Intendant Hocquart wrote to the French Minister ...

At times she was quite dutiful and obedient to the instruction given her by the priests, while at other times she was very obstinate. I cannot do anything but send her back.

No more was heard of this adventurous young woman. It is likely that she left New France. But to where? Perhaps she managed to find another way to freedom ...

No, this ship isn't going directly to France. First we head down the coast, to Louisiana.

Then we head across the ocean.

James Barry

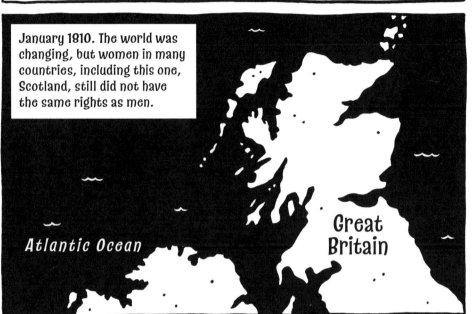

January 1810. The world was changing, but women in many countries, including this one, Scotland, still did not have the same rights as men.

Atlantic Ocean

Great Britain

Mother, I'd like be a doctor when I grow up.

Don't be silly, dear. Girls can't be doctors.

Aunt Mary Anne, I'm home!

Good evening, James.

Three more years of anatomy, surgery, botany, chemistry, theory and practice of medicine ...

Then I'll be the first woman to become a doctor in all of Scotland, maybe in all of England.

Of course, it will have to be my secret.

It's believed that James's real name was Margaret Buckley or Miranda Stuart and that James's "aunt" was really her mother.

One day you will go to the Royal College of Surgeons in Edinburgh.

The best medical school in the world!

But, Mother, with Father in debtor's prison, how can we afford it?

Even if people believed James was a young man, it was expensive to become a doctor. Possibly James was helped by an uncle, James Barry, who was a famous painter.

In any case, several friends of the artist were very helpful to the young person known as James ...

You'll join us tonight? I have several guests coming – artists, politicians, reformers ...

I wish I could, Lord Buchan, but I should study.

Several months later, James Barry graduated as a Doctor of Medicine.

Hello, James. And I must say, congratulations, *Dr. Barry*.

Thank you, sir.

How did he manage it? He's brilliant, but he's only 17!

I heard that Lord Buchan smoothed things out.

Women were not permitted in the military either, but in January 1813, James passed the entrance exam. However ...

You understand you must have a physical examination to enter the army?

Ah, sir, actually I wasn't aware of it ...

Is there a problem? We're running late.

Sir, you're extremely busy. You may take my word as a doctor that I am in excellent health.

All right, then. We'll forego the exam.

As you wish.

James Barry became a Regimental Surgeon, once again making history.

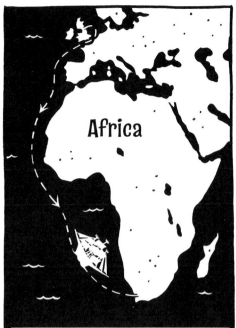

Africa

After working for several years in a British military hospital, 25-year-old James arrived in Cape of Good Hope, South Africa. Slavery was legal here. Those with money lived very well, but the needy were often forgotten.

The Cape was a British colony overseen by a governor, Lord Charles Somerset.

Ah yes, I've heard of this chap. Bright, opinionated, likes parties. And this letter from Lord Buchan recommends him.

Lord Somerset and James became good friends, spending a lot of time together in between James's many duties.

We'll head out to the leper colony now, driver.

Yes, sir.

September 1818. Lord Somerset contracted typhus. He was near death.

It's a message from the Inspector-General of Hospitals.

He disapproves of Dr. Barry's methods.

He is wrong. Tell him I will proceed with what I believe is the best course.

Oh, and, of course, thank him for his advice.

54

In December 1818, James became Somerset's personal physician.

March 1822.

James made it her business to visit leper colonies, prisons, asylums and hospitals.

I am Dr. Barry. I have heard that prisoners are being mistreated here, and I've come to inspect the prison's conditions.

No you will not, Dr. Barry.

Sir, this is a public institution. It serves everyone. As Colonial Medical Inspector, I am coming in to make sure it meets my standards!

Warden, what are these men eating?

Warden?

All right, you tell me.

Well, sir ...

James lessened the suffering of prison inmates and hospital patients. And she got rid of bribery and corruption.

James also spoke publicly against cruelty to slaves and in support of their rights to medical care. She tried to persuade politicians and business leaders to help the needy.

Of course, the poor have rights, too.

But her strong personality and forceful opinions also made her many enemies in high places.

In October 1825, James's enemies had her demoted. And in March 1826, her greatest supporter, Lord Somerset, returned to England.

In November 1827, the Colonial Office finally admitted James had been unfairly dismissed. She received a promotion to Staff-Surgeon of the Forces.

James left South Africa in 1828. She went on to serve in the Caribbean, in Malta and in Corfu. Everywhere she went, she was known as an outstanding surgeon, an expert in infectious diseases ... and an interesting fellow.

There's that extraordinary doctor.

And his latest dog. Each one of his poodles has been named Psyche.

Pillows ... we'll replace straw with feathers. Mattresses ... we'll replace straw with hair.

In 1857, James was posted to the British Empire's coldest colony, Canada. Within a year, she was promoted to the most senior rank possible, Inspector General of Military Hospitals.

59

Ellen Craft

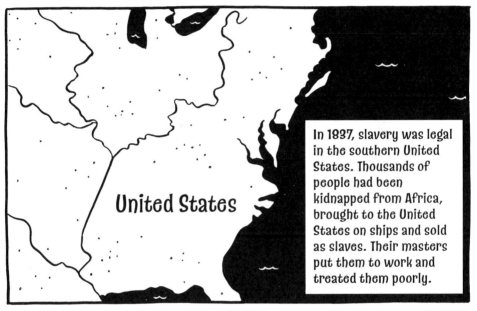

United States

In 1837, slavery was legal in the southern United States. Thousands of people had been kidnapped from Africa, brought to the United States on ships and sold as slaves. Their masters put them to work and treated them poorly.

Mama, I don't want to go!

Honey, you know you have to.

Ellen, an 11-year-old slave, was a wedding gift to the daughter of the family, the newly wed Mrs. Collins, who was leaving home to live with her husband.

Years passed as Ellen worked hard in the Collins household. Then one day ...

My name is William, William Craft. My master hires me out to earn some extra money.

Pleased to meet you. I'm Ellen.

Ellen's life was changed forever.

She and William fell in love.

Slaves can't even have an official marriage ceremony!

Our friends will be witness to our love.

Even after William and Ellen were married, they couldn't live together because they had different owners.

My skin is so light I can disguise myself as a white woman. I'll say I'm traveling north to ... visit a relative. You'll be with me as my slave!

It's been almost two years. I can't live apart from you like this.

Can't we take the money you've earned and escape north? Slavery is illegal there.

If we're captured, we could be separated. I couldn't bear that.

Well, our plan would have to be foolproof.

Ellen, it's too dangerous. You can't read or write, but most white women can. Plus, white women never travel alone with male slaves.

Well then, we'll have to think of something else ...

December 21, 1848.

This pass allows you to travel to the next town for the Christmas holiday.

Thank you, Dr. Collins.

But you must be back on the day after Christmas.

Thank you, sir.

Later that day, a Mr. Johnson and his slave were about to board the train.

YOU THERE!

Excuse me, Mr. Johnson. Can you please sign for your luggage?

Mnh-mnh. Ah don thing uh cahn.

Oh, that's all right, then. May I see your ticket?

Ah, on your way to Philadephia, then.

Run, Ellen!

No, we must stay calm.

This car is for white passengers. You ride back there.

Yes, sir.

Oh, no! It's Mr. Cray, my master's friend! He may recognize me.

It is a very fine morning, sir.

I'll pretend I'm deaf...

I said, GOOD MORNING, SIR.

hee! hee!

Yes?

I think he's deaf.

Indeed. Indeed. I'll leave him be.

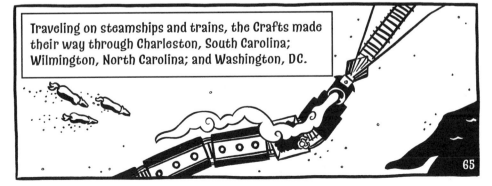

Traveling on steamships and trains, the Crafts made their way through Charleston, South Carolina; Wilmington, North Carolina; and Washington, DC.

When they arrived in Baltimore, Maryland, they found trouble.

I need proof that this is your slave.

But I don't have any proof.

Then you can't ride this train.

We're only one train ride away from freedom!

THESE TICKETS GIVE ME PASSAGE ALL THE WAY TO PHILADELPHIA, AND I INTEND TO USE THEM! NOW LET ME PASS!

William, we made it! We've traveled 1000 miles, but it's Christmas Day and we're in Philadelphia!

The Crafts fled to England in 1850. They worked with anti-slavery organizations for years and finally returned to the United States in 1869, four years after slavery was abolished.

Sarah Rosetta Wakeman

New York State, 1862. Disagreements about power and slavery caused eleven southern "Confederate" states to leave the Federal Government of America, or the "Union." The Confederate states and the Union states were at war.

Nineteen-year-old Sarah Rosetta Wakeman worked hard on her parents' farm, attending school when she could.

The oldest of nine children, Rosetta tried to help her parents by earning a bit of money working for a family in town.

69

In 1862, it was extremely rare for women to wear pants.

No one will guess I'm a woman! Now I can make a decent wage.

I'm not sure what to think of this.

I'm proud of her ... and scared for her.

In August 1862, Rosetta did "man's work" on a coal boat in upper New York State.

Hey, fella. You'd be better paid in the Union army.

The Civil War was one year old. Recruits were in short supply.

Luckily, the army's physical exam wasn't very thorough.

You look a bit young — short, no whiskers or voice change yet. But you're strong.

Good trigger finger. Now shake hands.

Strong enough to rip open an ammunition packet. He passes.

Good grip. And your teeth?

So far, so good ...

Yes, sir.

In July 1863, the regiment was assigned to barracks on Capitol Hill itself.

Rosetta enjoyed being a soldier.

"... I have got so that I can drill just as well as any man ..."

But she always feared discovery.

Can he tell?

I must take more care. From now on, I'll sign more of my letters with a man's name.

Edwin R. Wakeman

She had to act tough. When a fellow soldier picked on her, she fought back.

... so I gave him a few good cracks.

In 1864, the regiment was sent to the Red River Campaign in Louisiana. It took 10 days to march to Alexandria.

Here they joined other troops. Maybe Rosetta would have felt less alone if she'd known that hundreds of other disguised women were fighting on both sides of the war — including Jennie Hodgers, known as Albert Cashier.

Private Cashier?

Yes, sir.

On April 9, 1864, Rosetta went to battle on the front lines for the first time.

When will this stop? We've been fighting for hours!

CSA

The battle finally ended when darkness came. Rosetta stayed on the field until midnight.

Uhhh ...

Help me ...

On your feet, men. We're retreating.

Yes, sir.

They marched 40 miles back to arrive at Grand Ecore Landing on April 11.

Any casualties?

One in our regiment. 1300 in total.

76

Rosetta, like many other soldiers, developed chronic diarrhea. The trip to the hospital in New Orleans took 15 days. She was extremely ill when she arrived.

She died on June 19, 1864.

Sarah Rosetta Wakeman was buried as Private Lyons Wakeman. Her headstone is still in New Orleans, among 12 000 others.

No one knows how many women soldiers lie under headstones bearing the names of men.

Afterword

Kids hear "no" a lot more than adults do. And, unfortunately, throughout history and in almost every single country, girls and women have heard "no" more than boys and men have. "No, you can't do that." "No, you can't go there." "No, you can't study that." "No, you can't vote."

Women could not vote in Canada until 1917 (and 1940 in Quebec) and until 1920 in the United States. The first medical school for women was not founded in Japan until 1900, and women were not allowed into the American Medical Association until 1915. Women could not get pilot licenses in Canada until 1928. And NASA only started accepting female astronauts in 1977. It was not until 1995 that women could become judges in Iran, and it was only in 2003 that Pakistan began permitting women to train as fighter pilots in their armed forces.

Is it any wonder that so many girls have grown up thinking that their gender limits them?

But not all of them believed it.

This book is about seven women who just wouldn't, or couldn't, take "no" for an answer. They were born and lived within a wide range of historical time periods and cultures. Their tales will take you from 1470 BCE to the mid-1800s, from ancient Egypt to the American Civil War. Each woman was born into a unique set of circumstances and needed to conceal her identity for a different purpose: Hatshepsut wanted power; Alfhild wanted adventure; Margaret Buckley wanted a career; Ellen Craft wanted freedom from slavery.

Bravely, desperately, each woman made the same radical leap for freedom — she would change her name, her appearance, her identity ...

and "become" a man. There would be dire consequences if she were discovered; each considered the risk worth taking.

When disguised as men, they were treated differently by the people in their society. They were allowed to do more, say more, and they were given more respect than they had had as females. And, in each case, although all that they had changed was their clothing, they suddenly felt safer, smarter, more capable and more ambitious. Allowed the freedom to reach out and try, they could achieve their goals. Unfortunately, they had to do it while living a lie.

There are many more equally fascinating stories of women in disguise that just couldn't fit into the pages of this book, and it was great fun to research these "tales of daring women." At the same time, it was disheartening to have so many historical examples to choose from, so many girls who had to resort to subterfuge in order to follow their own path in life.

Today, there are still countries where men and women are not given equal rights and equal opportunities. In some countries, education for girls is considered a frill, not a necessity. Women continue to be more affected than men by religious and societal beliefs. Certain dress or behavior, such as wearing a bikini or simply traveling alone, might be considered "improper." And in times of war or upheaval, women are usually in much more danger than men of having their freedoms taken away.

It was, however, reassuring to find that more recent examples of women disguising themselves as men are harder to come by. More commonly, women are now being promised equal treatment by law, including equal pay, equal opportunities for education and equal rights to vote. In many countries around the world, women can become prime ministers and presidents; they can aspire to the highest levels of education and pursue the career of their choice; and they can earn good incomes and travel freely and independently.

I enjoyed writing about the adventures of these seven remarkable girls and women — and I hope you've enjoyed reading about them! I hope their unpredictable stories of independence and bravery persuade you to believe, as strongly as I do, that appearances can be deceiving. People should never be limited by others' assumptions about them. Everyone deserves an equal chance to reach out and try.

Further Reading

Hatshepsut

Hatshepsut: The Princess Who Grew Up to Be King

Read about Hatshepsut's childhood in Egyptian palaces and her journey to becoming pharaoh. Includes color photographs. Written by Ellen Galford (National Geographic Society, 2005).

Mu Lan

The Song of Mu Lan

A beautiful picture book translation of the Chinese folk poem "The Ballad of Mu Lan." Illustrated by Jeanne M. Lee (Boyds Mills Press, 1991).

Alfhild

Booty: Girl Pirates on the High Seas

A collection of true tales about real women pirates who sailed the high seas. Recommended for young adult readers. Written by Sara Lorimer, illustrated by Susan Synarski (Chronicle Books, 2002).

Esther Brandeau

Esther

A children's novel based on the remarkable adventures of Esther Brandeau. Nominated for the Governor General's Award for Children's Literature. Written by Sharon McKay (Penguin Group, 2004).

James Barry

With a Silent Companion

A children's novel inspired by the extraordinary achievements of Margaret Anne Buckley, otherwise known as James Barry. Written by Florida Ann Town (Red Deer Press, 2004).

Ellen Craft

5,000 Miles to Freedom: Ellen and William Craft's Flight from Slavery

The dramatic true story of Ellen and William Craft. Includes maps and photos. Written by Judith Bloom Fradin and Dennis Brindell Fradin (National Geographic Society, 2006).

Sarah Rosetta Wakeman

An Uncommon Soldier: The Civil War Letters of Sarah Rosetta Wakeman, alias Pvt. Lyons Wakeman, 153rd Regiment, New York State Volunteers, 1862–1864

A collection of Sarah Wakeman's letters. Recommended for young adult readers. Edited by Lauren Cook Burgess (Oxford University Press, 1996).